RAPTURE OF THE DEEP

Matter gave birth to a passion that has no equal.
The Gospel according to Mary

RAPTURE
OF THE DEEP

DEEP

Anne Szumigalski

Coteau Books

All poems © Anne Szumigalski, 1991.

Edited by Terrence Heath.

Paintings by G.N. Louise Jonasson.

Author photograph by Dark Horse Studio.

Book design by Shelley Sopher, Coteau Books.

Typeset by Val Jakubowski, Coteau Books.

Printed and bound in Canada.

The publisher gratefully acknowledges the financial assistance of the Saskatchewan Arts Board, the Manitoba Arts Council and the Canada Council.

The author wishes to thank: Canada Council for a senior arts grant which enabled her to complete this work: her many friends and colleagues who have given her advice on these pieces, especially Terrence Heath who edited the manuscript: and the artist Louise Jonasson for being so much in tune with her imagination.

Some of these texts have appeared in the following periodicals: *ARC*, *Prairie Fire*, *Border Crossings*, *Grain*, *Poetry Canada* and in the anthologies *Towards 2000*, *Out of Place*, *Soho Square III*, *Bridge City Short Story Anthology*, and in the Polestar *Writers' Calendar 1991*.

Canadian Cataloguing in Publication Data

Szumigalski, Anne, 1922-
  Rapture of the deep
  Poems.
  ISBN 1-55050-022-8 (pbk); 1-55050-023-6 (bound)
  I. Title.
PS8587.Z44R3 1991   C811/.54   C91-097149-8
PR9199.3.S986R3 1991   76984

Coteau Books
401-2206 Dewdney Avenue
Regina, Saskatchewan
S4R 1H3

For Andris,

from whose conversation many
of these pieces arose.

CONTENTS

Notes

THINK OF A WORD

Think of yourself thinking of a word.

You are standing on a beach at sunset, looking out over water that is neither choppy nor calm. Small waves are flapping against the shore, breaking up the brilliant light that is falling upon them. Nothing is a sheet of colour: not the furrowed beach: not the streamered sky: not the flaked water. Should your glasses slip or your head itch, you will take no notice; you will not move. Your stillness is precious to you. You refuse to listen to your own breathing. For wouldn't that be an admission that parts of you, at least, are moving? You refuse to see the possible swimmers in the water, the probable children on the beach. You shut your ears to their cries, to the voices of the fathers who may be calling to them. "Alone with the sea and the sky . . . ," you keep repeating in your head. Is the word then *banal*? "Unchangeable as a star . . . ." Is the word *commonplace, burial, denial*? For the stars, now faintly prickling the sky, do indeed move.

They are just now rushing away from you, the Earth and the Sun, simply because all these are abhorrent to them. You, in fact, are the centre from which they are fleeing. A weak centre at that, one who cannot even remember whether this is the ocean or simply a very large lake. Great Slave comes to mind. But in those western waters there are many white stone islands, islands with smaller lakes within their rocky boundaries, which lakes contain their own little islands, and these islets have their own ponds, and those ponds each its own tiny jutting rock, centred by a puddle of rainwater. All of these islands are dirtless and treeless. The lake is full of fish, and the quartz is full of gold. Sunflecks fall upon the water and seep into the rocks. Or are they simply tarnished by the failing light?

At least this: the word is not gold. If these are lakewaters they are grey eastern ones, the kind you have long ago learned to despise for the sludge that runs into them from hundreds of greasy rivers. It is dusk with a last thin green streak in the West and a last heavy sigh, which is the sound of the descending sun, and now you discern in the greying light a skeleton caught on a distant sandbar, perhaps the bones of a large fish, perhaps the bleached remains of a small child.

This red planet, a wet crab, has just dug itself out of the sand and come upon your feet and challenged them.

Slippery, brittle, ambidextrous? There is nothing to say that the word must be a noun. Is a crab ambidextrous? Not surely when one claw is so much larger than the other. But isn't that simply because they have different functions? What if both functions demand equal skill? Crabclaw so meloncoloured. Can the word be *melon, seed, oceanography,* or should it be *skiff, sail?*

The man in the boat holds high the lantern. He brings the small craft about, kills its motor, and neatly beaches it. Meanwhile, you have had the presence of mind to fling yourself down on the beach and play dead, the rising crabs and sandfleas nipping at your belly. With deliberation the man steps out of the boat and slowly walks around you. You're still as a rock, holding your breath, not daring to count the seconds which seem so long and impossible. You won't give in. Nor will he. He tries to turn you over with a strong, rope-soled foot. He leans over you and sniffs for the stench of death.

At last, a laugh breaks open your tight lips and runs out over the dark beach. He laughs too and takes off his jacket and wraps it around your shoulders, as you stagger up groggy in the chill.

Now he seats you in the bow of the boat, hands you the lamp, and shoves off. You stare glumly into his ruddy face as he pulls at the cord, not turning away as he does so, but staring sternly back into your eyes as though, if he had his way, he would condemn you to wander forever, like the saint, from word to word, from island to island.

JESUS

A child sees Jesus coming towards her through the glass of the nursery door. When his reflection fades, she turns around, and there he is standing right behind her. She knows him by his beard, by his pierced hands, by his bare feet, cold on the linoleum. He bends down to kiss her, and she notices that his crossed halo stays there on the wall above him empty, waiting for his head to fit back in.

She's pleased with the visitation of course, but she'd much rather he'd sent an angel with long feathered wings to lift her up and fly with her over the tops of trees, over oceans full of rocky islands with seabirds nesting on them.

Her mother has warned her that he is simply a man, with all the things a man has: bristly chin, hairy knees, bony feet, this and that. Sooner or later, her mother has said, he will come for you and take you on a long journey.

The child glances outside, and sure enough there is a very old donkey with downtrodden hooves tethered in the garden. The scruffy-looking thing is chewing on some lilies in the perennial border. Spotted orange petals and black tipped stamens are scattered about on the grass.

Jesus has his arm around her now and is urging her through the door and down the path towards the back gate. Panic, like a long-necked bird, is opening and closing its beak in her throat. Nothing comes out, not even the crumbly hiss of a murrh.

She looks back at the house, at the nursery door still standing a little open. "I should go back and shut it," she says to the man who is squeezing her shoulder with large possessive fingers. He doesn't answer, but points with his other hand towards the road, where she sees her mother getting into her small yellow car. She has on her big straw hat, the one she wears for picnics. Her father is already sitting in the passenger seat. He has taken off his glasses and is breathing on them, first one side and then the other. Just as the car moves off, he holds them up to the light and begins polishing the lenses with his large, white pocket handkerchief.

AN ACCIDENT

Outside, a man is suspended. More daring than any lumberjack, he hangs there polishing the windows of the 36th floor.

"How is it that I dream always of the woods?" he asks, "where everything is so tall. Ah, those straightup roughskinned pines! Ah these squat oaks of concrete!"

"Good day," he nods to me. "Now you can see clear across town."

And yes I can, and I look in at a window, a quarter of a mile distant at least, hoping to see you bathing our child before a small wood fire. You holding him over a cracked enamel basin; I pouring water on his head from a cup. This is how we baptized him, in what may have been another country, another century.

Yet your arms are still bandaged from the accident as you sit down at the piano in your wide, light room. Your arms are bandaged, but not your hands.

Nothing could harm them, the music explains. And your fingers run along the keys like mice in their winter tunnels. Then your mouth opens in the serious grimace of a song. It opens. It closes. And your elbows move up and down. Believe me, I feel the scabs, which have stuck to the dressing, tear from your skin.

Now, in some inner room, the child awakens, and at once you try to temper your song to his mewling. Oh, oh, you sing, my skin falls away from me like dry leaves. My forest of aspens stands blackened. My lake is floating with charred fish.

How fearfully your fingers hammer on the instrument. How hunched are your shoulders. How low your head hangs over the keyboard. And flecks of blood, smaller than cinders, begin to colour the loosening bandages.

THE ELECT

Here in the saintly dark, all is so cleanly dank, all is ordered and cradled. Nothing is sinful. Even the suck of the worm's mouth upon us is preordained, therefore right.

Suddenly, it's dawn up there. It comes with the silver squeal of birds, a sound like thin trumpets. "Crack the box," it says. "Arise, this is the day."

Obedient as buds, our heads appear in the open grass, and a rain of golden yods falls down upon us. So this is light. We had forgotten it.

We, who lay long in holy depths of earth, have all at once become small and new, can't even remember our names, and the passers-by won't tell us. They stop. They smile. They stare and then move on.

At last a child in blue cotton leans down to us. "Daffs," she says, and, taking each of us by the neck, yanks for the love of God.

THE DOVE

It troubles the boy that, if you want to draw a white bird, you must use a black pencil — or, at least a dark grey one. A drawing can never get away from its hard outline.

His aunt promises him that tomorrow she will buy him black paper and white chalk, and he can try again.

"No," says the boy obstinately, "for when the sky is black it is night, and no one can see anything, not even a white bird. You can hear the whirr of her wings as she passes. That is all."

"Perhaps," suggests his aunt, "it could be moonlight."

It's bedtime, and the woman places the drawing on the nightstand beside her nephew. Then she kisses him and leaves, shutting the door softly, but decisively, behind her.

The boy puts his hands over his eyes and pretends to sleep. Through his fingers he can just make out the drawing peeling itself from the page and flying away into the dark. The bird has abandoned him to his dreams.

During the long night, the child comes to the understanding that the bird is in some way his mother.

The drawing itself, he knows, is his own creature and must obey him. The bird, on the other hand, is free to follow all her whims and desires.

It is morning, and he wakes to the closed-in light of snowfall. Barefoot and tiptoe on the cold roses of the linoleum, he stares through the window. The garden and the road beyond are a single space of trackless white.

On the sill he notices a small curved feather. It could have come from his pillow of course, but maybe his aunt has placed it there, in hopes of comforting him a little for his loss.

Suspicious and grave, he takes up his crayons and gives the bird her colours: glossy yellow wings, an emerald poll, a blue breast speckled with red.

The bird is now more splendid than his mother ever was. Pinned to the paper with the brilliance of her plumage, she will never be able to escape again.

GREY

We women sitting in the downtown bus on our way
to buy new duds for an event which should have
been foreseen but however long you wait for a day it
always surprises you with its sudden coming the
calendar speeding up when you're not looking and
none of us wants to find herself in last year's finery at
a whitwalk or picnic where we are to be admired our
coiffes neat as helmets of dried-out curls thin on top
which we try to hide with the help of various Mandys
and Terris for why should we do it ourselves at our
age haven't we earned with our years something a
little special at least once or twice in a grey moon
shading to foxy red or brassy with a tint of dust about
it.

Later in the church hall kitchen catching up on the gossip behind a wedding just now being celebrated with thump of feet and sweat and jello in plastic dishes with a dab of ice cream on top melting milkly into the raspberry like the world upside down and the white sea melting into the red sun which of course it has long ago done for us ladies whose only good now is the proof of our hard work on such occasions as this our not believing we have worth in anything but the number of steps taken or juicy glasses and plates stacked or if we make the best mashed potatoes in the bunch which is hard to do as with all this practice we are every one so very good at it for we believe in the salvation of food given and taken and floors scrubbed and beds turned down at the edge for infrequent visitors from out of town yet still we grumble happily over tea on the days we allow ourselves the indulgence of a bus ride to go shopping and not to one of those goodworks meetings which are so many but varied of course to give everybody a change from the church there are societies for visiting the sick those other more decrepit women lying sourly in their beds in nursing homes all with the names of the bishops who laid the foundation stones places which far from subtly let it be known that they'd rather not accept those of another religion but will do it at a pinch to prove goodwill among christians and jews and other stranger faiths which wouldn't happen here if only they had kept to the immigration laws of long ago which we all agree were much kinder to all concerned in the end for there was far less tension in those days and now everybody is so violent you have to be careful going out at night no matter what part of town you live in.

And so back to the bus where we sit side by side knitting tiny sweaters and bonnets even occasionally something for ourselves so as not to waste time there is so little of it left but what there is wearying and long not many miles to go but the foolish fellow at the wheel he drives so careful and so slow.

HALINKA

It is right, they say, to bury a stillborn child with a mirror on the pillow beside her. That way, at the resurrection, when she opens her eyes for the first time, she will see her face and recognize herself.

But that's not for you, little daughter, little flaccid creature. For you, there never was such a thing as a face. There were hands and fingers, curled feet with curled toes. There was a heart in your chest, red and whole as a candy, and a white iris growing in the place of your understanding.

AFTERNOON

One rainy day a woman sits writing at the kitchen table with her wrists sticking out from cotton sleeves that sag slightly over the page where words are arranging themselves in the shape of trees and shredded tailfeathers of peacocks which lie scattered beneath them there in another country where the voices of children can be heard shouting over the din of traffic about a restaurant looking over the water where you can wind out the winkle's flesh upon a pin all the while noticing the tide erasing your footprints on the sand below you sitting there with the knowledge that if there is a storm you are quite safe for it can't get at you behind the tempered panes of the windows and the door through which comes the woman's neighbour taking her boots off and sitting in the other chair asking for advice about her husband and the muddy season of fruits and vegetables going rotten which the woman cannot answer but never mind says the friend most of the answers are in here anyway and she takes her new calculator out of its zippered pouch and explains its functions and progressions which lead to a blinking of its red indicators when it's asked the wrong question which of course the woman does and the neighbour impatiently snaps up the shades and they just sit there watching showers of mud splashing up from the wheels of cars as they rush past in the rain which goes on and on like snatches of a song that keeps recurring in the woman's head about a distant sea in which plankton float not the usual minuscule kind but giant stars and spirals wider than cushions finned and brittle.

Dr Basalt and Reza are suited up for the dive. Breaking the surface with their backs, they tumble down towards the centre, intent on measuring the mud below the sea: sand, pebbles, silt, gravel, clay.

Dr Basalt believes that under this part of the ocean, beyond these five barriers, he will find traces of a forest burned to the stumps more than twenty million years ago. Reza believes in Dr Basalt, his old sinewy strength, his evident wisdom, not of the World but of the Planet, she is fond of telling people smugly. She is young yet, and her legs are firm and strong inside the wetsuit.

She digs down with a small shovel, laughing because it's so much like the toy spade she used to dig sandcastles with at age five. Dr Basalt takes things more seriously. With a silver tablespoon he's filling the special plastic containers with samples from the different levels. But, every time a hole gets down to level three, it collapses in on itself, taking the sea and the seafloor with it.

Reza wonders, will the whole ocean be sucked down to the Earth's molten core to be lost forever? Or could there be some place over on the other side where it would all pour out, no doubt destroying a fertile plain with its salty flood.

Try again, Try again, the old man signals, for he's desperate to find the streak of ochre which will signify the lost forest, not to mention the tiny fragments of charcoal, which will attest to that forest's destruction by lightning-fire. It's obvious that he desires this evidence more than anything else in life.

Reza doesn't need any encouragement, for her own purpose is strong, though quite different from Basalt's. She is longing for the end of things. "Omega, omega," she whispers to herself, as she digs bravely on.

She doesn't look for a fire to put out, but one that will never be quenched (at least not for several billion years). They are far from the Rift, she knows, yet, if she could dig quickly enough and deep enough, might she not uncover just a small hairsbreath crack in the crust? Perhaps there will be a moment's flash in the bottom of the next hole, and, for just a second, she will be able to contemplate the fires of eternity from the safety of her vigorous young body, and the protection of her mentor and his scientific attitude.

When at last they are hauled up, it is obvious they have stayed underwater far too long. "I was betrayed by my overweening enthusiasm." Dr Basalt explains, blaming himself for Reza's bends.

Now they will have to spend the night in the decompression chamber, dressed in loose blue cotton gowns to allow for swelling. "Not more than ten percent," explains the medic, as she clangs the door shut behind her.

It is pleasantly warm and light in here, but there is not much to do. A couple of decks of cards and a few fashion magazines are all that has been provided for their amusement. There is also a large black cat. By way of a chaperon, Reza wonders.

Or could this be some kind of experiment? This makes her uneasy. After all, have we the right to involve another species in this kind of thing? She writes a quick letter in her head to the SPCA. Dear Madam or Sir etc. . . . . cruelty if not physical then at least mental . . . flagrant lack of respect . . . who do we think we are, God or something? . . . yours etc. Reza Kalmer (graduate student). Meanwhile, the cat curls up on the bench next to Dr B and purrs itself to sleep.

Not that he notices it for he's engrossed in a game of solitaire. Reza watches him sharply for a while, but, to her disappointment, he never once cheats. If she were to fall asleep like the cat, would this change? Would he give in to his lifelong passion for answers and solutions? Reza has noticed, that in his work, he sometimes gets impatient with the facts and fudges things a bit.

What shall she do for her own amusement? Should she pick up the biscuit-coloured phone and ask for bagpipe music, or a midnight snack? But then it may not be midnight. There is no way of knowing in here. In the end, she is forced to play the same old game she always does last thing at night.

In the game she imagines a whole shelf of books. They are old books with faded cloth covers, and the titles, which were once stamped in silver and gold, are now a spotty grey — quite illegible. The rule is that she may pick any book, but, once chosen, the whole thing must be read right through. She runs her fingers up and down the row several times before she chooses a chunky volume with a watery red cover, the kind that will stain your hands if they are in the least bit damp. Even a bit of sweat will do it.

When she opens the book, it is, of course, the very one she always gets, no matter how carefully she picks another colour, another size.

It's the same old story: an outdated account of the shrimplike creatures which flourish in the almost boiling water that wells up in the ocean over the eruption of an undersea volcano. The magma pours out of the glowing crack, hardening almost at once into lava pillows which pave the seabottom like enormous cobblestones.

The heat hatches the little creatures, which rush upwards determined to break through the surface of the ocean and experience air, that beckoning poisonous element.

Luckily for them, the skin of sea is too strong to be broken by their tiny heads, and down they float once more mating and shedding eggs as they go. The poor things are dead before they reach the seafloor, where they are eaten by any hungry scavenger that happens along. But each minute exoskeleton (and this is the part that affects Reza the most) is spewed out to become just one more particle of the detritus that covers the seafloor.

Always Reza surprises herself by not being bored with this tale. By the time she shuts the imaginary book she is, as usual, almost in tears. She looks up, and there is Dr Basalt patiently at his game. Now she realises that the flap flapping of his cards is the sound she has been hearing all through the story. Somehow she had mistaken it for the restless and endless movement of the sea.

A GRACE

In the beginning, we put everything into our mouths. This was through fear. The satisfaction of the nipple had nothing whatever to do with it.

Each one of us had to encompass her own terror, so that it became small as a horse swallowed by a maculate python, creatures we never see nowadays. To us, they are little more than legends, little less than myths.

Great Grandmother was one of the last of those barbarians who bit into warm grey loaves burned in an oven and smeared with a kind of grease got from the milk of tamed cattle.

Think of it, they even chewed the flesh of those beasts. Fibres of meat got caught between their teeth, which in those days were brutish and white as fangs.

We praise then this food set before us, these subtly coloured piles of light delicious dust arranged on iridescent glass. An elegant waiter, wearing the tall blue hat of a son of the *chef des chefs*, has poured the repast through white paper cones. The result is a landscape of decorous pyramids, which we delicately suck in through silvery tubes, giving thanks for our simplicity, our victory over ourselves.

For we have been given the grace to overcome the crass impatience of our kind, are willing to wait out the seasons, until the fragrant orange falls to fragrant dust, until alfalfa powders itself, and beans in their mottled glory crumble.

As the wind blows, and time moves the molecules from place to place, may we ourselves, our bones, become spoonfuls of ivory particles in the mouths of our descendants, our children's children's children. AMEN

ENTERING

She's decided it is time to admit to her dreams. She will write them out morning after morning in a blank book, one she's had for some time and has so far not found a good use for. The book has a tweedy cloth cover with grubby corners and edges.

She decorates the top of every page with a row of pencilled faces, their eyes shut, their tongues stuck out derisively. The faces have no ears and their noses are nothing but a couple of uneven nostril dots. At the bottom she draws a line of houses, each with a pitched roof, two windows and a door. The doors are tight shut and there is no smoke scribbling from the chimneys.

I didn't do this on purpose, she writes in the back of the book in a section marked NOTES ON FORM. I was just doodling, and so I suppose the faces to carry nothing more than the simple meaning: dreams I have dreamt and am happy to forget.

The houses, she admits, are a different matter altogether. For certainly, no one has ever yet entered them. She has no desire to be the first to find herself standing on one of those untrodden coco mats, turning the fine iron key in the brass lock on the white-painted door. For then, she'd be certain to dream that behind that door there are no rooms, no walls. She will find only a patch of thorny garden sloping down to a grey ocean, whose many mouths suck on the cold stones of the shore.

is telling how the princess won't eat chocolate biscuits any more. Nowadays, she has digestives with her morning cup of tea; all because she thinks she's too heavy for a young woman her age, especially her breasts are too big. But what can you expect, says Des, so soon after?

We are sitting at tea ourselves, and why do we always get these HRH stories at every meal? Mostly it's the little children, how they grow and develop princely ways quite soon, and wear silk romper suits and black patent shoes with buckles in the shape of coronets. We imagine them peeing into golden potties and sleeping in high white prams among the roses of the palace gardens. Swallowtail butterflies flit about their heads, now and then touching a wing to a baby cheek, but never so roughly as to disturb the royal nap.

Mother says, "Nonsense. They are just like you but not nearly as well brought up. The spoiled little things are given over early to the corruptions of wealth and station. Quite soon caterpillars of doubt will begin to gnaw at their souls, just as our garden caterpillars gnaw at the growing hearts of cabbages."

Des does her best to counteract these heresies, though she has to admit you wouldn't believe the goings-on of the bachelor brothers and cousins. Ah, what a relief for the whole country when they marry and settle down and have their own little royals to worry about.

As for the HM's and the RD's, they, of course, are far too august to be the subjects of casual mealtime chats. We know them only from pictures Des cuts out of magazines and pastes into her scrapbooks. She keeps these in a drawer in her room and brings them out for us to look at on special occasions only. There are the ladies sitting about on spindly chairs drinking, sometimes tea, and sometimes sherry from glasses like crystal crocuses. They have to sit up straight all the time, Des explains, so as not to wobble the stiff little crowns resting upon their perfect grey curls.

The kings and dukes, on the other hand, always remain standing, it being obvious their trousers are much too tight to be sat down in. Their right hands are poised on their sword hilts, and their old, but manly, chests are buttoned into splendid military tunics and decorated with rows and rows of medals. "Quite unearned," mother points out bitterly. Only the gold oakleaves on their collars show any signs of modesty, half-hidden, as they are, behind pointed white beards.

AS SO MANY DO

The day starts bright as a songbird. Later, it turns grey and begins to drip. Wings of clouds mantle the town where melancholy grass is beginning to turn yellow at the roots.

It was a day like this I had a fit of grief on the bus so that my tears wriggled down my face like rain on window glass. The man behind me tapped me on the shoulder, offered a blue cotton handkerchief. The woman beside me dug in a damp paper bag and handed me one of those sugared doughnuts that are so gritty and hard to swallow.

Afterwards, I noticed I had accepted the young man's arm. I leaned on him as we walked homeward, his shoulder wet with my sorrow. Or was it simply the drizzle dampening every surface?

When we reached the house I wouldn't let him go, and so he sat down beside me on the bed limply smoking. After a while, we both dozed off, bundled and sinless as I thought then.

I awoke to find he had taken off with several of Harry's things, which were still lying about the house — a pair of pigskin gloves, two antiquarian books, and a black silk umbrella.

Now he might have needed the brolly, but what could he possibly want with rare books, a man I didn't even know the name of. I made enquiries. He wasn't a local boy.

On dark afternoons like this, I open the curtains wide and sit obviously reading under the soft light of the lamp. Surely the rain will return that stranger to me, he of the cool consoling hand, he of the light fingers.

FRENCH AND ENGLISH (a game)

The French are quite right about their language. Even in these polluted times, it retains a certain purity. Even when it is translated into English, its stringent nuances shine through, as the incorruptible corpse of a saint shines through a shroud.

Or, perhaps, it is a tower standing in the middle of a field, a tower strongly and delicately built of white marble. A good many men, and lately some women, dressed in splendid uniforms, guard the tower night and day.

English, on the other hand, is the feral field itself. Once cultivated, it is now overgrown with weeds and wildflowers. Very likely, this is because the farm keeps changing hands, and every husbandman has his own ideas how things should be run. What one sees as neglected land, another views as summerfallow. It is at the point now when nettles are growing in the hollows, and one part of it has been used, on and off, as a garbage dump. There is even a dead donkey in one corner. The poor thing has been lying there for some time. Flies are buzzing round its head; birds are pecking at its eyes. Poor old English donkey.

Time passes, and the flesh of the donkey becomes maggots, becomes grassroots, becomes raven's wings. Tell me, which language would you rather speak — stone tower language or dead donkey language? Don't forget the flies.

THE CRANES

The interior sounds the body makes — how do they escape to the outside air, to ears other than our own, though we try to close every orifice? We make sure the eyes are lidded, the ears plugged, the mouth and other sphincters puckered tight. That leaves just the nostrils and they, of course, are continually busy, taking in and pushing out small gulps of air.

And haven't we all heard of the woman whose infant wailed in the womb? She got up to go to him, but could not find him, though she searched the whole house. At last, she remembered he was within her, kicking and crying from the other side of her flesh.

As for me, too late have I resolved to keep myself to myself. Though my fluids may leak out, I'll take nothing more in. The result of this must surely be an inner desert, as arid and gritty as the great sand hills, where in summer cranes walk and call. In autumn, they gather in the dunes and fly south to another desert, even hotter and drier than this one. And somehow, when they return, there is always one left behind, alone as I am, crying out against the solitary fate of females. But why should I need other companions, with this child lying in the crook of my arm, his closed and veiny eyelids, his mouth sealed with a soft white smegma.

How pale he is, barely breathing. There is only just time to awaken him before his sleep slips into an internal state. Before the sound of his cry is lost to this world, and to me who invited him into it.

PURPLE

It's the backend of the year. Purple loosestrife wands stand black and dry in the garden. We can hear their papery scratching above the traffic, below the gusting wind.

The chaffy seeds fall as we watch. Who could believe the urgency of that scattering? More than a poet desires fame, or a traveller his bed, each one of these seeds desires its own resurrection. But why should God, who after all did not heed the desperate prayer of his only Son, spare even a moment's thought for a loosestrife seed?

Nevertheless the seeds do not give up. With their innocence, with their patience they beseech Him night and day. They think of their rustling as a voice repeating over and over, "Be ashamed, O God, be ashamed of your dryness, your lack of words. How is it that the very wind speaks, but you do not answer us?"

After several weeks of drought, their Lord at last allows the rain of His mercy to fall down upon them. Most of the seeds drown in this sudden outpouring of love, but a few simply float it out and are saved. After the flood abates, these manage to take root in another part of the garden. But things are not all that good. The soil is soggy and cold, and fine white worms crawl up from the mud and feed on the delicate new leaves. The seedlings feel they have enough evidence to lodge a formal complaint.

God sends a mediator, an angel with double qualifications, she is both a botanist and an ecologist, to deal with their foolish arrogance. Come, come, she says, you must agree that we can't allow the whole garden, let alone the whole planet, to find itself twenty inches deep in purple loosestrife.

Well how did she figure that one out? Can she, a mere angel after all, have come to understand the relationships of all created things? Of course not. Like the rest of us, she has just enough knowledge to deal with the question in hand.

As always, the long winter allows us to forget the existence of purple loosestrife until March, when you and I find ourselves sitting knee to knee before the hearth, leafing through the garden catalogues.

To our surprise, no mention is made of seeds. However, there are vivid descriptions of many flowering perennials, including loosestrife, in several shades of pink and purple. Instructions for planting the carefully divided roots are given in great detail. On the back cover of every catalogue is a nicely designed order form with the cheerful slogan: GOOD LUCK WESTERN GARDENERS IN THE COMING SEASON.

ANOTHER QUESTION

It is quiet and glum at the grief meeting until V gets up to speak. He tells how the other day he had opened a closet in the basement and god had fallen out in the guise of a vacuum cleaner, old-fashioned and out of use for ages, and of how this brought to his mind the dusty carpets of his youth: the green like worn turf, the glaring gold with pink roses, the unsatisfactory wall-to-wall that had to be torn up and carted away to the dump.

"Does this prove," he asks, "that creation does not exclude even the most footling of our artifacts, or perhaps simply that there is more rubbish strewn on the path of evolution than we have ever dreamed of."

Well, I for one can stand only so much of this kind of thing. I decide to leave immediately for the railway station, for I have always taken solace in that place, where the soot rests calmly on the bricks; it has not, after all, been disturbed for more than a century.

The journey is a weary one, for the train stops at every station. Not only that but we are sidetracked every time we meet with a freight on its way to a useful, V would say a productive, life.

"Get on with it. Get on with it." I yell from the open window of my compartment, for I'm anxious to be home and unlock all my drawers and closets. There I hope to find undisturbed dust and the powdery scales of long-dead moths and perhaps grains of sea sand from a forgotten holiday.

What is my chagrin, when I at last turn the corner of my road, to see V standing fresh as a lettuce under the streetlamp by my gate. He is obviously anxious to test his latest theory on the relationship between grit and sorrow. Before he can get in a word I challenge him: "What has all this to do with that ridiculous Tuesday group meeting at the Ministry," I say, "you know as well as I do there's not even a doormat in that stuffy little room, nothing but uneven vinyl tiles in a colour between brawn and snuff."

Even this doesn't nettle him. He speaks not a word but takes my elbow and guides me through the door of my own house. "The way we are destroying each other," he explains, sitting me down at the kitchen table and filling the kettle for tea, "reminds me of nothing so much as a forest, whose trees have grown so old that their roots are entwined, tightening year by year until they kill each other."

"Aha," I reply, "but there are still the beetles, those tiny deities, those flakes of omnipotence. Little by little they carry away the deadwood for their feasts in the underworld. When they have eaten their fill, I believe they will have mercy on us, for after all they are the only ones who can answer our constant question: When will the forest give way to desert, the desert to sea, the sea to forest again?"

KNIT

she takes the bus downtown to buy clothes to wear in
this city of women where they pump water by night
and by day they knit sweaters and stockings chatting
on the streets because what else is there for the hands
and the eyes or for the bitten tongue so long and pink
and fresh-looking in spite of its age the teeth of
course are young they are made one day and the next
they are buried still smiling ah what a waste of ivory
and porcelain and pink plastic shining there under
our feet so mind your step ladies and your best nylons
mind your hundred and forty-nine dollar silklike
print it's just such a pity when you think of all the
knitting that went into that purly cardigan soon to
ravel unseen in the damp of the earth

VIATICUM — THE TEXT

On the first morning, we saw a road stretching before us, and this road was one long word reaching from here to there. How enticingly clear and simple this seemed. At once, we packed bread and cheese and knives and skins of fresh water and set out with a will upon our journey.

At the close of that day, the road and the word came to an end, and we struck camp for the night. On the second day there was another road, another word. And so it went on. However, at the end of the sixth day things were a little different. Because we had stopped on our way to pick the serviceberries that grew by the side of the road, we arrived late at our camping place. It was already dusk, and we were so tired that we threw ourselves down on the grassy verge without as much as taking off our boots or washing our faces. Indeed, we were so tired that we even forgot our evening prayer to our creator, the Demiurge Y, he who had undoubtedly arranged this journey for us and watched over us as we travelled.

When we awoke, the midmorning sun was hot upon our upturned faces. Above us, in the blue dome of the sky there was not a single cloud, simply a sentence made up of all the words from the past week. The message was simple and direct. As soon as we read it, we fell into momentary despair, for, up to then, we had thought ourselves innocent, or almost so. Truly, we were not deserving of such a judgement.

There was no road and no direction. Would there ever be again? Here we were in the wilderness with no one to guide us. Though our hearts beseeched the Demiurge, he did not heed us. Well, there was nothing for it but to make the best of things, and so we lazed through the day in the long fragrant grass. Even the insects joined us in our rest, and nipped at our skin so gently that we hardly noticed their bites.

Of course Y did not allow us more than one day of rest. The next morning we were off again pursuing the word and the truth with a little less enthusiasm than before, yet still curious to know where the road would eventually lead us.

Now the pattern was set, and we continued for what seemed like centuries in the same way. On every seventh day the week's words were added to those already crowding the sky, and every sentence was more difficult and threatening than the last one. It was not surprising that the Demiurge had decreed a sabbath of rest. We could imagine that it could take him a whole day to compose a suitably abusive judgement for the next week's journey.

As for us mortals, we were glad to stop on the road to fill our flasks with fresh spring water and to enjoy the scenery and the warm sunny weather. When cool evening fell, we began our sabbath dance, watching the shadows of our gestures move gracefully under the moon.

Y was obviously not at all pleased with our lightheartedness, for his words became every week more forbidding and his path more rigorous. In some places it was overgrown with thorny weeds, and in others it was ankle deep in stinking brackish water. Our creator had made up his mind that we were to travel among the sharp stones, grasping at stinging nettles, and even at poison ivy if we were so foolish as not to recognise its trinity.

One Wednesday morning, as we were wandering along a flinty road that passed through a rock strewn valley, the enamel sky, which must have become overburdened with the many curses and judgements written upon it, cracked and split into a thousand, thousand pieces. One moment the sky was full of words, the next flakes of blue were falling upon the earth like scurf from the unwashed heads of angels.

And these flakes floated down upon the grass and the stones and the hills and the rivers and the bitter oceans. They alighted too on all the birds and the beasts, even upon our friends the insects. And from this falling all creation received its voice. Never was there such a roaring and a twittering and a buzzing and a squealing. As for us poor wanderers, we too received this blessing. Our ears and our mouths were opened, and we shouted and sang and argued until our throats were sore.

Now there could be no more sky words, and no more need for us to travel the earth. This was the place of our deliverance. We made up our minds to settle in this spot and to build a city with the stones that lay around us. Here we live still, passing the days in discussions and quarrels and the evenings in the singing of bawdy ballads and the telling of tall tales.

No longer are we confined to gesture and the written word. Indeed we have almost forgotten how to read and write so happy are we with the speeches and lies which come effortlessly to our tongues.

As for our master the Demiurge, he has been defeated by his own cruelty and arrogance, for he among all beings did not receive a voice. The sky of words fell downward only, and Y was far too proud to descend from his heaven and accept the gift of speech. In his high place he is silent still, though every now and then he throws down his orders and curses in a written scroll or codex. Of course, we never read these for we are far too busy chatting and boasting and reciting for that.

However, we are not entirely lacking in piety. In the very centre of our city we have built a modest temple to contain these holy objects. Sometimes one of our children, with the natural curiosity of the young, demands to learn to read and to discover the secrets locked up in those pages. Then we gently explain that our revered creator, Yaldabaoth the Demiurge, has promised to punish with terrible severity the impious fool who dares disturb the dusty silence that lies forever upon his words.

[37]

A SANCTUARY

There are women living in a house on the mountain, a house that sticks to the rocks as tightly as lichen. At dawn they come out on the bluestone ledge. They stand in lines, a choir singing us awake. Their high voices in unison are a sort of shriek, hard for the teeth to bear.

We look up, and they look down upon us poor primitives in our deep valley not yet enlightened. Look, we say to each other, how cold it is up there. The snow scuds around their feet like an ankle veil.

Snow which hardly ever falls in our valley. If we wanted we could grow potatoes all year long. When it's a bit chilly, we chop down trees and light small fires. A few snowflakes fall into the flames and sizzle to nothing. And perhaps our smoke rises to those holy nostrils, and perhaps it brings tears to those holy eyes.

When we have too many girl children, we send a few babies by rope to those women above. We bundle the little ones in quilted bags, for we don't want them bruised as the sisters haul them up the broken face of the rock.

They say that on the mountain no one has teeth, for there is nothing whatever to chew up there. Ground bones of their dead is what they eat, and sometimes powdered reindeer moss. It's rumoured they suck these delicate meals through straws of ice.

None of us has ever climbed the mountain to speak with these women, for how could we hope to comprehend their wisdom? But we do sometimes stare at them through a makeshift telescope, trying to tell one nun's face from another.

And sometimes a lowly farmer will put his ear to the mountainside, straining to catch the voice of his lost child in prayer, as she kneels in her granite cell, whispering through her puckered mouth cool words of separation and of grace.

THE FLIGHT

of angels: the sough of air through their feathers: the fanatic beat of their pinions: the celestial honking of their song. Either they have just passed over or they are about to darken the morning with the wings of their thousand formations, each with the head of Azrael at the arrow's point. Their necks outstretched, they rush past the clouds like geese in autumn, like swans in the spring.

But these do not travel to the North or to the South. Westward only they circle the planet, scooping up this one and that one. Our souls that leap from the body are gathered to them, to nestle in white down. As lice on pelicans, as mites on cranes, we infest the holy pink skin of angels.

THE FALL

My father was born in a distant country where every person is a tree — every adult that is.

Children are fieldflowers, they are grass, they are lilies and poppies and small blue lupines. Until puberty, they are any plants they choose. More than that, they may change their minds as many times as they wish. A child may wake as a gillyflower and go to sleep as eglantine. Is it any wonder that, in that country, no one is in a hurry to grow up?

At the age of twelve or so, each must name a tree and is stuck with this choice until the tree falls from age, or is struck down by the axe of the woodcutter. This last is their way of explaining the death of the young in battle, for, in spite of their worship of the peaceable plant, they are a warlike lot.

All this my father told me, but though I bothered and cajoled him, he would never say which tree he had chosen or whether, in this new country, he still felt bound by the customs of his birthplace.

He always seemed just a man to me, and very like other people's fathers: that is, strong and infallible in my childhood and, as I advanced into adolescence, more and more clumsy and overbearing.

There was one difference though. Unlike other men he was never seen without a shirt or a sweater. Not that he was particularly modest in other ways. Several times I caught him pulling on his trousers in a hurry. I had a good look. Nothing strange there. But what was he hiding beneath his T-shirts and button up cardigans? Was he afraid of woodpeckers? Was there a hole there, beneath his heart, where a squirrel had made her nest?

I was almost a grown woman when he took me for a holiday in a warmer part of the country. It was May and already early summer in that gentle climate. He pointed out a tree I had never seen on the Prairies and acknowledged it as his own. *Hippocastanum* he explained proudly. Its leaves were huge green hands, and between them sprung tall racemes of bloom like white and yellow candles. This then was my father's tree, generous in its spread, amazing in its summer complacency.

We stood there, hand in hand, as he told me about its various phases, of how in fall it would bear inedible brown nuts in leathery green cases, nuts that are the weapons of little boys in their battles.

All this was years ago, and my father is dead now, hollowed and fallen like every tree before him. I was with him when he died.

No sooner had he taken his last breath than I leaned over him and began to unbutton his pyjama jacket. What did I expect to find? Simply the chest of an old tired man, the tangles of coarse grey hair intricate as twigs, the nipples hard and resinous as winter buds.

Speculation comes easily to the man who can't tell the difference between this and that reality. His habit is to accept or reject each day, as though it was nothing more than a scrap of roasted lamb, offered at arm's length, on the point of a knife.

Often he dreams of severed limbs, but is never quite sure whose arms and thighs these once were. He has decided it doesn't matter. He likes them like that, unattached, flung far from what lies at the centre. Far from this head, whose mouth speaks endlessly, as though it might be a sin to leave a breath's pause on the tape.

It's only when he's gone, the one distance, the one direction possible, that we can bring ourselves to play the whole thing back. And then, of course, he seems to speak to us out of another time. But is there more than one?

That was always his question, and now that he's out there, it's natural we should think of him carefully gathering up the dust of his bones, for every atom of this white grit must be fitted together before he can begin on the flesh, his answer.

His wife dries her tears on a napkin of leaves, and lies with his brother under the open sky, calculating the propinquities of genes. For her there is no extension or bending of the light. Her desire is to get on with this life. But first she must find, in the depths of heaven, his one clear abiding star.

So perfect is her longing, that she has forgotten the iron pot, left balanced over the campfire. By now the hunter's stew has burned to the metal.

All night the lovers scrape and scour. Will they never be able to divide one substance from another?

$$i^2 = -1$$

A chocolate egg is made by binding two equal halves together.

When it is whole, balance it on the pointed end and spin. Eventually it will waver and fall on its side (but which side?) and roll. Never again will you be able to tell which half was right, and which was left.

Or indeed whether the egg is divided N/S or E/W.

But it's true, isn't it, that before something has become a whole we may not refer to it as divided? The trick of a word, the sag of the language, may mean it has always been whole, even before the two halves were joined. Apartness. Agglutination.

Invent me a set of pure symbols. Write me a letter in unmistakeable signs. But are these signs unmistakeable from each other, or are they simply unmistakeably signs?

Now give me an imaginary number; speak me an imagined word.

Resurrection. The tomb opened. An egg broken cleanly, perfectly apart.

You are four-and-a-half, and the eldest of three girls. When you look in the wardrobe mirror in the bedroom, you see a stout person with sturdy legs and a cloudy face. That's because the glass is scratchy and pitted just there. Never mind, your mother says, by the time you are six you will have grown so much your face will be clear as midday. Your chest will be in the dim though. Does that matter? Not a bit. There's no girl of six really interested in looking at her chest.

You are tall for your age, your father often says, and a strong sensible person. Everyone calls you The Big Girl.

Besides Big Girl and Little Girl, there is the new baby. They have decided her name will be Rosie, but you just know they'll always call her Baby, until the next one comes. Perhaps the next one will be a boy and not a disappointment to your Da, like you, and Little Girl, and Baby Rosie.

And then there's Granny Oakes, who is still in the house from the birth. She always calls everyone by their real names. "Bring me a nice dry nappy from the pile on the blue chair, Dorrie love," she says. "Now watch how I do this. When I'm back home in Shropshire, you'll have to see to the baby sometimes for your mother. She'll be weak awhile yet. Watch how I put my finger back of the nappy, so as not to prickle little Rosie." "What if it prickles *me*," you ask. She laughs at you. "You're much too big for that," she says.

There are five chairs altogether; three in the kitchen, and two in the bedroom. All of them have piles of baby things: nappies, nighties, soakers. And when you look up you can see more of them, hanging on a rack far above in the rafters. You can see your mother's great big nightgowns too, with the round pinky stains that haven't washed out properly. Looking at the stains makes you feel kind of sick. You remember how Mum screamed when the baby came. How the District Nurse told you to go for a walk, "and take your lunch with you." To go right now, "and run will you."

You sat on the hill with your back against the big tree and listened to the wailing from the house. Somehow it hadn't seemed fair to Mum to go any further away than that.

After the crying stopped, you fell asleep on last year's leaves and acorns, and you didn't wake until Granny Oakes came calling for you and said, very softly in your ear, that you had a new baby sister. A bonny little thing. You couldn't help wondering why she kept wiping tears from her cheeks. "Is Mum dead?" you asked. "Of course not, you little ninny," she said. You felt bad about that. It was almost the only time Gran had ever been sharp with you.

To make up for her crossness, she had shown you how to work the pulley for the clothes rack. First you unwind the cord; then you let it go, and down it comes, with a whoosh and a squeak. You have to be careful though, not to let Mum's nightgowns drag on the floor.

When Gran isn't changing the baby, she's washing out this and that in the scullery. She stands at the sink in her bare feet, singing songs from Ginger Rogers films in her high pretty voice. At least that what she says they're from. You have never actually been to the flicks yourself.

Da doesn't care a bit for cinemas, or for Gran's singing either. He says she is frivolous, whatever that is exactly. He has a long pale face and big teeth. He says Lord Jesus gave us voices to sing His praises in chapel. You like to sit on his knee sometimes and talk about God, and things like that. It's different from everywhere else. Sitting on Da's knee is a world apart. On Saturdays he is teaching you your letters. By next year you'll be able to read the words of the hymns, he promises, perhaps even some texts from the Bible. Grandmother Evans, he tells you (that's his mother that's gone to be with Jesus already) could read the Bible when she was three years old. Just some of it, and not to understand, of course.

Little Girl is away at Auntie Mary Jenkins'. She wouldn't be much help anyway. She still wets the bed and howls when Da spanks her for it. She smells of wee, and her knickers droop down below her frock. "Untidy," says Da, "I don't think, do you, that's she's going to grow up into a serious person." You ask him what's a serious person, but by now his nose is down in a dark green book with the back torn. You ask him again and again, but he doesn't answer, except to tell you to buzz off and give Granny a hand.

Granny Oakes has wrung out all the nappies she was washing. They are in a pail on the brick scullery floor ready for rinsing. Gran and you carry the pail between you out to the pump. You love helping her work the pump, though you do wish the water would come a bit faster. "It's a good thing you're on the heavy side," she says, as you jump up and drag the handle down. For a minute, it nearly has you off the ground, but it gives way just in time and, after that, it gets a bit easier. Squeak, squeak, it goes, a nastier squeak than the clothes rack, but still a squeak. All at once, you know you like things that have a noise to them.

It would have been worse if there'd been silence when the baby came. You forgive Mum for screaming. It's one of those times when you understand everything that ever was, when everything is one thing, and the cracks and spaces between them are only lines, like the ones on paper when you draw pictures.

Gran has finished rinsing and wringing, and you are handing the pegs for the clothesline. It's funny, but the smaller you are, the more washing you make. Little Girl makes a way more washing than you do. And as for this baby.

The work's finished now, and Gran, after a quick look round, hoists up her skirt and takes something out of the pocket in her big pink bloomers. It's a little bottle of blue glass. "Is that poison?" you ask, thrilled and horrified at the same time.

She laughs and throws herself down on the grass and reaches up and pulls you down beside her. She takes a swig, then wipes her mouth with back of her hand. "A bit of the dandelion is all," she says, and takes another swallow. You just sit there watching, while her cheeks get rosy, and her eyes begin to sparkle. "Your turn," and she hands the bottle, "you're a big girl now." You tip the bottle to your mouth, just like she does, and you watch the sun shining through the blue glass dimly, like in the woods, or in chapel when it's bright day outside. She hasn't left you more than a sip or two. It's sweet and warm, as you drink it down.

You and Gran are lying side by side now, laughing and singing the Ginger Rogers songs. You just sing la, la, la, because you don't know any of the words. Then, all at once, up gets Gran in the middle of a song and starts brushing the bits of grass from her skirt. "Time for your Da's tea," she says. "Now mind, turn your head away and don't breathe on him. We're lucky, both of us, that he's not the kissing kind."

THE OPENING

She has worked it all out, what the child will say when he is born. "Basket of harvest pears," he will say, "Waterfall of pearl. Sky of zircon." And, looking up, "There's a fly in the sky," he will say.

She wonders what she will answer, but doesn't worry about it too much, for she has always believed that words will come in their time.

But when at last the child has struggled from her body, there is an age of silence in the room. She props herself up on her elbows and sees him lying there, grey as plaster between her legs, his mouth stoppered with a plug of slime.

Her shriek hits the air and breaks it. It falls like shattered ice upon the woman and her child, who swallows the mucus with his first breath and reddens from his crown to his heels.

"I am," he says.

"Hold your tongue," he says.

"Woman, what have I to do with thee?"

THE BOY AT THE UPSTAIRS WINDOW
WITH HIS HEAD IN HIS HANDS

it is heavy as a stone he tells himself like any rock in
the field of rocks on grandfather's farm where
boulders are born out of the prairie every spring if
these are the heads of huge stone infants where are
the bodies to follow narrow from shoulder to toes
after the round agony of the head or could they be
ancient skulls that the earth gives up a thousand
years after their burial what with the rain and the
wind something must surely come to light in the end
for this is in many ways the field of jesus the place
where he decided to make an end of his journey he
who had travelled as far as india and back he who has
been seen in every city in the world at one time or
another just walking around stirring up trouble
many times thrown into jail for disturbing the peace
of such places as this where the bones of the earth
break up and are carried away by farmers who make
piles of them in the corners of every field and dear
are these rockpiles to the child they are his moun-
tains and ramparts and sometimes he sees brilliant
snakes slithering in the cracks the rocks also are of
every colour and grandfather says if you split one of
these suckers you could find a coiled seashell or a
perfect fern or perhaps just a hollow place the boy
understands that this hollow is the very same secret
room where he lives always alone tracing the
mysterious maps on the walls with a wetted finger
trying to find how to get away from cartoons of
rabbits and cats in hero's hats to where fair ladies are
advertising the subtle gifts of the mind

[51]

FOXED

What the old woman looks for in any drawing is the crosshatching, those triangles and lozenges so like the fine lines on the back of her own hands, which a little soap and water will erase for a minute or two. Not so the rusty stains; they always remain, though she spends her money unwisely on creams and lotions which promise that in three weeks or so the damned things will disappear into the background beige of aged skin.

These are the same blotches she noticed as a child in the old etching hanging on the nursery wall. It was of an angel, his arms outstretched over two children perpetually teetering on the edge of a cliff, and he forever hopelessly trying to prevent the fall.

PASSOVER

This is the burden of the solitary prisoner, eating alone like a dog at his dish. And, for lack of a companion, he is eating himself. For every man needs to share his grey hunk of bread. There he sits getting neither fatter nor thinner, and it's always Friday Dinner with no candles to light. It's always an evening in June, drawing in so very slowly towards dark.

Outside a dog is chained to the shadow of his kennel. A woman bends before him, offering an enamel plate of scraps. The dog cannot hide his disappointment; he has waited so many years for an invitation to supper. Every night he wonders, will this be the day of deliverance, when I'll sit up at the table with my paws on the white cloth, waiting for my portion, waiting for Father to fill my cup with milk.

For surely by now they have forgiven my attack on the baby, how I leapt upon her snarling and worrying. That was long ago, but still this tether is a chain of events, one leading inevitably to another, and yet one more.

But then, is it possible for a prisoner to turn his crime into triumph? Is it possible for a dog to cease longing to be a man?

THE ISLANDS

It is the fate of those who live on the mainland to long for islands. Not so much lake islands, those snatches of land entirely surrounded by weedy water, which water is entirely surrounded by trees and sheep pastures. And there is no littoral. No, most of us desire sea islands, and whatever journey we take, they are our true destination.

I

From our aircraft all we can make out is the fog that hangs over every island. The pilot explains that this mist is simply descended cloud, and that beneath this white barrier are scraps of grassland, peaked hills, rocky cliffs where only seabirds visit. I yearn for an island that is nothing more than an oak forest. You seek an atoll where harsh fruit falls from the palms onto the sand beneath.

Looking through gathering darkness across the width of the sea, the captain at last spies an island clearly visible. The fog has lifted to show the City of Faith surrounded by the waters of unbelief. There is no countryside — simply a high wall and a shingle beach, upon which the waves batter from age to age. "Behold Hierusalem," he says over the intercom, "hidden so long from our eyes."

II

One day, I take a taxi down to the docks to a place marked on the map as *The Isle of Dogs*.

Sure enough, while I hide in a close overgrown with roses, five dogs go by dragging five men on leashes. These dogs are small, but how powerful they are! None of the men can withstand the violence, the patience of their pull.

From their window in the attic above, three young women look out pathetically. No wonder, for they have no dogs, not even one between them. Every day they arise before daybreak and scuttle off to work. Every evening they return after dark to a meagre supper. After they have eaten they play loud rock to chase away the blues.

"One day," the youngest says as they prepare for sleep, "we'll have saved enough to buy into the puppy market. Oh, then we shall be / so happy and free."

III

Minds, some small as toy balloons, some huge as sky islands, float over the world seeking what each craves — a much convoluted brain about the size of a grapefruit.

Each of these minds has a leash dangling from it and, at the end of this, a set of small sharp teeth, which it clamps into tissue as grey as the sea. The teeth of the mind are glassy, invisible.

A child is playing in a meadow when she looks up and sees one of these parasites dangling above her. Without a quibble she believes it is hers, and she is its. Somehow it has persuaded her that it is a matter of love, and that, if she accepts its invasion, that terrible joining, she will in some way become its mistress. She even agrees to take it to school with her, foolishly imagining that a bit of training will make this thing obedient as a dog.

Minds are everywhere, waiting for a chance to leap upon any of us, and most of us give in and let them have their way. Still, there are some who resist, by an act of will strengthening their meninges until they are as tough as horseleather. "Idiots, idiots," we smugly call after them. And the idiots smile, delighted and uninhabited.

IV

Lately in a dream, I was visited by an island. As it neared, I saw it was full of roses and unexpected animals. They lived in houses, and each one had a man chained to his doorstep to watch and to cry, "Stranger, stranger," when another man approached.

Without waiting for an invitation, I stepped ashore and saw at once that I had been deceived, for this place was nothing but a field of weeds. There were no dogs, no houses, no men. What could I do about that? Night was coming on, and I simply lay down amongst the groundsel and the wild poppies.

When morning broke, I disembarked and walked away without a word. In my inner ear I could hear the voice of the island as it floated off. It told me that it would return. It never will, of course. I was so cold to it.

The nun / midwife tells a certain young mother that god has truly blessed her, for she has been chosen to bear quintuplets. What an honour!

But the woman weeps, picturing the litter of infants lying within each other's curves, every which way within her womb.

"Foolish girl," the nun says, "dry your tears. You are not carrying all these babes for yourself. One is for you, the rest are for us sisters, the holy ones. They will be ours and ours alone, until the time comes to give them back to the Pleroma."

The mother dreams of hiding her children in places where the light cannot touch them. At first in the drawers of her bureau, later in the thick woods behind the house. In her dream, she covers them over with dark veils, sometimes of cloth, sometimes of matted leaves.

"Nothing can be hidden from the Immutable," explains the careful midwife, as she swaddles the babies in white bandages. One at a time the nuns carry them out to the car. "Here, this one is yours," and Sister Superior turns at the door and tosses the last child onto his mother's lap. "If I were you," she says quite kindly, "I would call his name Jesus."

her face is plain in the english style called pudding-
face blameless as a sweet bun with currants for eyes
and a thin satisfied smile pasted on with watery
white icing and I ask myself why are you so attracted
but no wonder for it is remembrance you are after the
sun and moon waned long ago the girl as she must
once have been her squarish figure her thin shape-
less legs *beautiful as a cranefly* you murmur as for me I
view the whole thing quite otherwise for I think her
now as lovely as she has ever been nostalgia is not for
me just a simple prayer o madre you who sent her let
her stay only as many days as there are petals on this
simple flower not that it is your fault for who can tell
when love will strike

the clock booms out five and we sit down one each
side of the garden table the third chair being for
herself when she has served us as it is her place to
carry out the china cups and milk and a mahogany
tea bitter as sansevieria and more potent at last she is
done o how slow the poor thing is the stream pouring
from the spout took nearly as long as her recitation of
the joys of mary for she has been brought up in a
convent and must be allowed her little ways but you
are not for grace are you love as for me I am for letting
the words fall into the teacups and cause those coins
of bubbles that mean money in the purse daisy
promising to look into this when time permits how
can you take a person like that seriously

now it is my turn and I dutifully borrow her white
lace cap and apron and fetch out the hot scones and
jam which we all eat with gusto though yours is
restrained by your obvious crush on the woman even
though her plaintive voice fills the air with tedious
explanations of why all things come together in the
most unexpected ways at the most inappropriate of
times

god bless this teapot she intones even though you and
I are not finished with our eats you licking the last of
the strawberry jam from the spoon and I gathering
up the crumbs from my plate with a wetted forefinger
— *and all who pour from it* — as she is the one doing
the pouring this seems a little excessive as does my
foolish riddle *what does the letter el stand for?* surely
there must be an answer but we are all silent then
daisy gets up and one at a time tosses the leftover
dregs from each cup into the bushes

LEXIS

You awake with a word in your mouth, one you have never tasted before. *Copt*, it says, *Copt*.

It smacks of strange metals, of what's left behind after a draught of familiar apple juice. You can't decide whether this taste is delicious or hateful. Yet you know very well that eating the pith would have saved you from this dilemma.

Copped, you repeat cleverly. *Yes, I suppose I have been.*

But you cannot outwit the desire of the word. Use a *K* it advises sweetly. That way you'll always get my meaning. Repeat after me: There's a Kopt Knocking at my Kryptic door. Let him thrust his Key into the Keyhole. Let him turn it and enter. He will not be turned away.

GERALD

The spiritual advisor, he told us to call him Gerald, commanded us all to kneel. Most did so, but a few of us held out against a demand we felt to be humiliating. Then we were to put our hands on our heads as a token of submission. None of us did that. After all why should we debase ourselves simply to please a power-hungry old man?

We were surprised when we heard his ancient cackle of a laugh, astonished when he praised the rebellious ones. "Obedience can be a sin," he explained, "in certain circumstances." We imagined a circle within which the more timid of us were trapped, but others ran boldly about and were not confined by any particular system of thought.

It took us only a day to realise that in fact we had all been bamboozled, for if we were disobedient again then it could be concluded that we were confined by our need for praise, our slavish desire to please the hierophant. That's how we regarded him now, simply as an old teacher of orthodoxies, with all sorts of tricks up his sleeve to catch out any of us who leaned dangerously towards independent ideas.

Nothing, we knew, had changed since our world began, this small world of our studies, our constant striving towards the light. The path is dusty and the road is thorny. We knew that of course, and we accepted as inevitable the sharp stones of Gerald's disapproval as we became a group united against the holy old reprobate.

He would try to conquer us; we would resist him. We held secret meetings to discuss all sorts of ways of cheating him. Maddingly he appeared to take no notice, "All these little venial sins are of no importance," he seemed to be telling us. Indeed he forgave us everything. He beamed indulgently upon us. Can you imagine how infuriating this was? After all, we had not come here to be pandered to, like a bunch of silly children.

It was then that we decided to separate. Perhaps we had misunderstood the dictum, *divide and conquer*. Each of us took a different road to the destruction of the old man's argument. We forgot the words, *united front, common purpose*, all that sort of rubbish. We were no longer a pack of wild dogs nipping at his ideas. Each of us became his own creature. We even went so far as to wear badges to denote our differences: a tiger, an anaconda, a scorpion, a fierce but elegant rogue elephant. This last was of course myself. I felt huge wearing that badge. But I knew as did the others, that we were now not just contending against our sainted master, but against one another. We were each as likely to injure another student as we were to hurt His Reverence. Could a tiger, I constantly asked myself, leap upon the back of an elephant and sever its spine with one bite? If I, the elephant, were to step upon the scorpion would her sting prove mortal to me, as my tread would certainly be to the venomous little arachnid?

Thus had the sly old master divided his enemies. Now he could conquer us one by one. We would not even want to call upon each other for help. Nothing could save us from the cage, the circle, the swap and the sellout.

And so he has won our souls, and we are obedient to him, though not slavishly so. For Gerald has left this world and left it to us, his students. As we watch an old woman grinding his bones on the mountainside, we are brought to the realisation that his dust and the taste of it pervades all of us. We eat him, we breathe him, we take up into our own bones the Geraldessence which will certainly divide us and pollute us, as much as it will bring us together and makes us one.

If O had not told me I would never have guessed that the two rows of chairs tipped up against the table, the board, represent the members of the ultimate government, all of whom, he explains, are permanently absent.

"But isn't there a chairperson, a speaker or a speakeress?" I enquire. "O foolish woman," says Owain, "don't you know that in this place there is neither male nor female? The person or personage who holds the chair, that big one at the end with carved armrests, is simply the one with the biggest bottom. The way you are going on — and he gives me a friendly pinch — you may qualify yourself, that is if you agree to having your breasts nipped in the bud."

Once long ago, he tells me, he had addressed the Board. He was young and foolish at the time, and did not notice that the chairs were empty, and that the great armchair at the head (or was it at the foot?) of the table was filled, as it always is, with nothing more than bluster, fury and unction. And a demented sense of having been insulted.

So the chair is Rod the Pole on his Perch? I am mortified that Owain is too busy to notice my clever pun. He is in fact impertinately lowering his backside into the velvet upholstery of the august chair, almost a throne. I can't help wondering how he manages to be sitting there and, at the same time, standing humbly before the imagined President bowing and scraping and addressing the Grand Master in a convincingly whiny, and yet arrogant, voice?

"O Great Progenitor," he intones, "You who first planted a garden. The days were fine. The nights were cool. The mornings were dewy. Everything grew and flourished. Not for you the weeds and the slugs. Your magic eye would zap them if they ever raised their heads. Not for You the withering drought, the twisters that raise up the dirt behind the tractor and carry it far away to other fields. What do You know about growing a decent crop in this dust dry place? We all of us have the advantage of You there."

"That'll teach Him not to tip back his chair," remarks Owain aside. Then in a stage whisper he begins to tell me of this secret cave where a council of equals meets all unbeknownst to the Great Chairman. Like most such get-togethers this one finds it difficult to come to any decisions, but the speeches are good and so are the intentions. "We meet every Saturday of the year," he boasts, "and there we sit, at a perfectly round table, with our cups of coffee before us, talking, talking, talking."

THE FISHES

There's a woman lives up north in the forest who knows how to call up creatures from the lake.

They say she came from some place on the coast where she lived out her youth amongst the Finnys and the Clams. And now, in her middle years, she's moved in here to bother our lake. A foreign woman who has no business in this place.

Whenever the fancy takes her, she stands on the beach with her toes in the water and gives a sharp scaly whistle. "Come to me, you darlings of the deep," she sings. "Come up and recognize me." And they do. They rise up upon their silvery tails and dance over the water to her, and tell her all their secrets and troubles.

"Fishland, after all, is very like our own country," she explains. "People get depressed, so do fishes. All does not go swimmingly with any group of creatures. Even men and women whose children trail after them in the dust."

What does she do in winter, we all wonder. Surely, she doesn't expect those slippery creatures to break ice to come to her. "Not at all," she says, "I behave like everybody else. I have made myself this little house on skids. I drag it to the middle of the lake. I augur a hole. I call them and they come. In the winter they have few troubles and so they just sing fish songs and tell stories of anglers they have lured into the water with their wiles and tall tales, upon whose drowned bodies they feed for months at a time."

And does she never deceive her fishy friends, we ask. "Of course," she answers briskly. "There's always one foolish enough to jump into my frying pan. How delicious he is with a pinch or two of salt."

NOTES

ANNE SZUMIGALSKI

Anne Szumigalski has written six collections of poetry including *Woman Reading in Bath* (1974), *Doctrine of Signatures* (1983) and *Dogstones* (1986). She has also collaborated with Terrence Heath on four radio dramas and on the poetry collections *Wild Man's Butte* (1979) and *Journey/Journée* (1988). In addition, her poetry has appeared in countless Canadian and international journals and magazines. Her poetry has also been published in numerous anthologies, most recently *Out of Place* (Coteau Books, 1991), *Soho Square III* (Bloomsbury, 1990) and *Towards 2000* (Fifth House, 1990).

Over the years, Anne has won many major literary awards and prizes including two Saskatchewan poetry awards, two Writers' Choice Awards and two nominations for the Governor-General's Award. Anne received a Founders' Award from the Saskatchewan Writers Guild in 1984, was named "Woman of the Year" by the Saskatoon YWCA in 1989 and was honoured with the Saskatchewan Order of Merit and a Life Membership from the League of Canadian Poets. Anne has read in many locations in Canada, several in the United States and in Great Britain, including Oxford University. Anne was born in London, England and immigrated to Saskatchewan in 1951. She currently lives in Saskatoon.

ABOUT THE ILLUSTRATOR

G. N. Louise Jonasson was born in Winnipeg, Manitoba where she presently resides. She received her formal education in fine arts at the University of Manitoba, completing her BFA Honours thesis in painting. In addition to several solo shows, her work has been included in many group exhibitions. She has participated as a mentor in the Mentoring Artists for Women's Art (MAWA) program and as a board member for PlugIn Gallery. She continues to work as the visual arts editor for *Prairie Fire* and devotes most of her time to painting. She is represented by Melnychenko Gallery in Winnipeg.